Step back in time with the PM dinosaurs as you learn NSW Foundation style handwriting.

My name is

My teacher's name is

My learning goals and success criteria:

- I can trace and write all lower-case letters of the alphabet in NSW Foundation style.
- I can trace and write all capital letters of the alphabet in NSW Foundation style.
- I can trace and write all numerals 1 to 100 in NSW Foundation style.

Are you ready to write?

Posture

Is your back resting against the chair?

Are your feet flat on the floor?

Paper position

left-handed

Are you holding the paper steady with your non-writing hand?

right-handed

Pencil grip

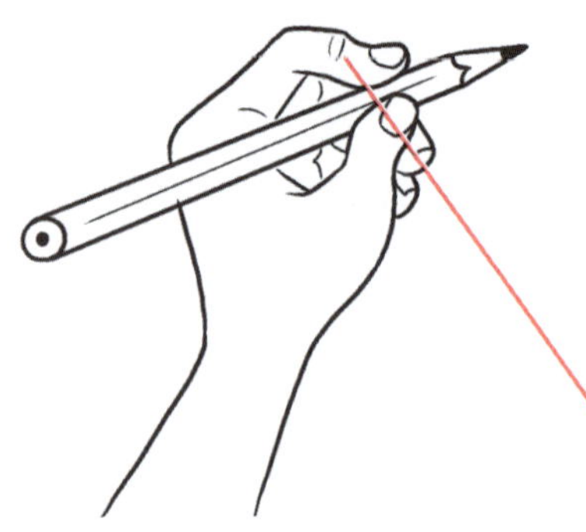

Is there only one finger on top of the pencil?

Left-handers, hold your pencil a little further up so you can see your handwriting!

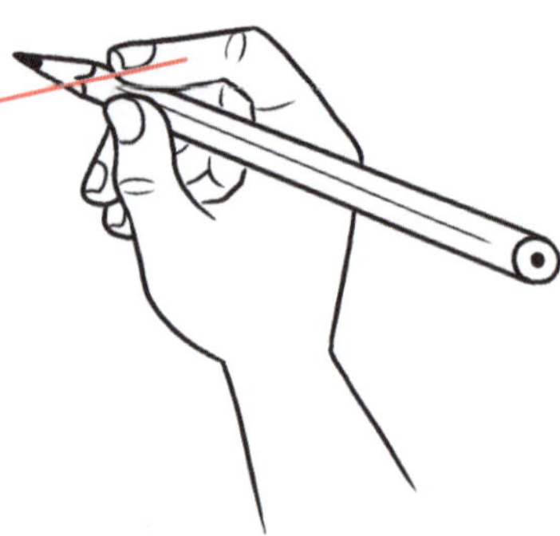

1, 2, 3, 4! Are my feet flat on the floor?
5, 6, 7, 8! Is my back up nice and straight?
9, 10, 11, 12! Show me how your pencil's held!
Thumb and pointer side-by-side, lucky tall one takes a ride!

Anti-clockwise movement

Try these anti-clockwise patterns. Start at the dots. Follow the arrows.

Trace.

uu uu uu uu

Trace and copy.

u u u u u u

u

U U U U U U

U

up underneath unroll untied

Which letter have you traced or copied the most carefully?

Find your best lower-case 'u' and place a tick neatly above it.
Do the same for your best capital 'U'.

Trace and copy.

Q: What do you call

Q:

a clever dinosaur that

never gives up?

A: Try–try–tryceratops!

A:

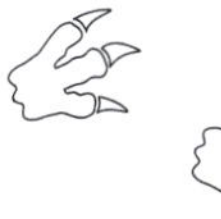

Trace.

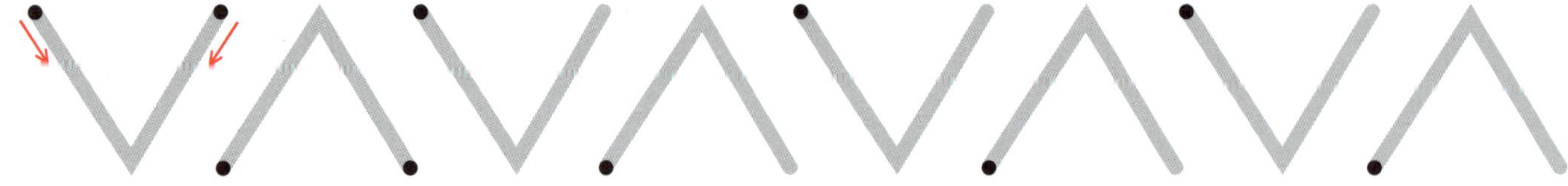

Trace and copy.

y y y y y y

y

Y Y Y Y Y Y

Y

year young yesterday

Find your best lower-case 'y' and place a tick neatly above it.
Do the same for your best capital 'Y'.

Trace and copy.

Many years ago, a young dinosaur came out of his hole. Little Dinosaur was looking for adventure.

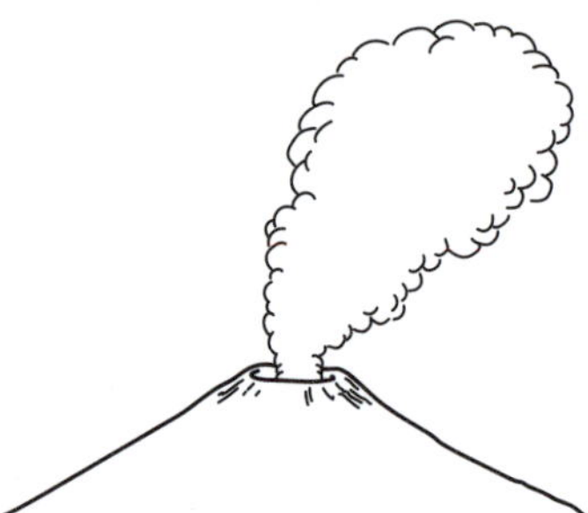

Trace.

vvv vvv vvv vvv vvv

Trace and copy.

v v v v v v

v

V V V V V V

V

volcano village lava very

Find your best lower-case 'v' and place a tick neatly above it.
Do the same for your best capital 'V'.

Trace and copy.

Rivers of hot, red lava

came down the side of

the volcano.

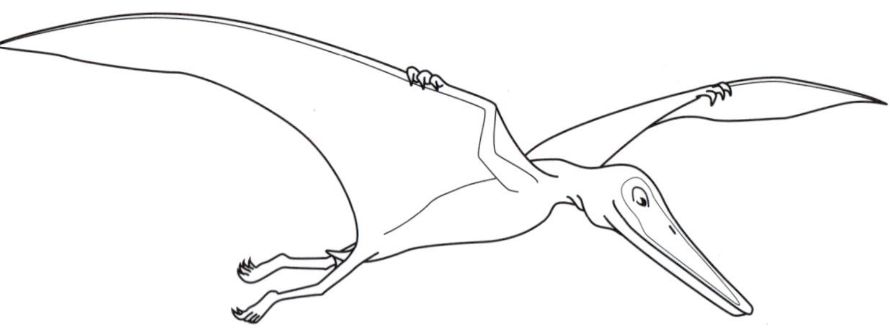

Trace.

Uul Uul Uul Uul

Trace and copy.

w w w w w w

w

W W W W W W

W

was what wingspan

Find your best lower-case 'w' and place a tick neatly above it.
Do the same for your best capital 'W'.

Are you ready for a dinosaur fact?

Trace and copy.

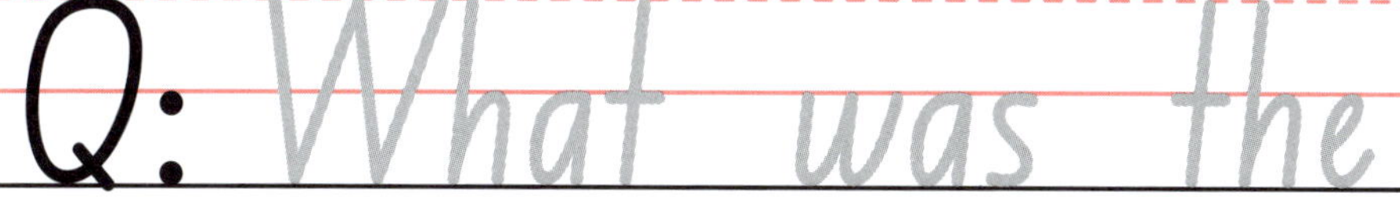

Q:

wingspan of a pterosaur?

A: About 4 + 2 + 3 + 2

A:

= ______ metres long.

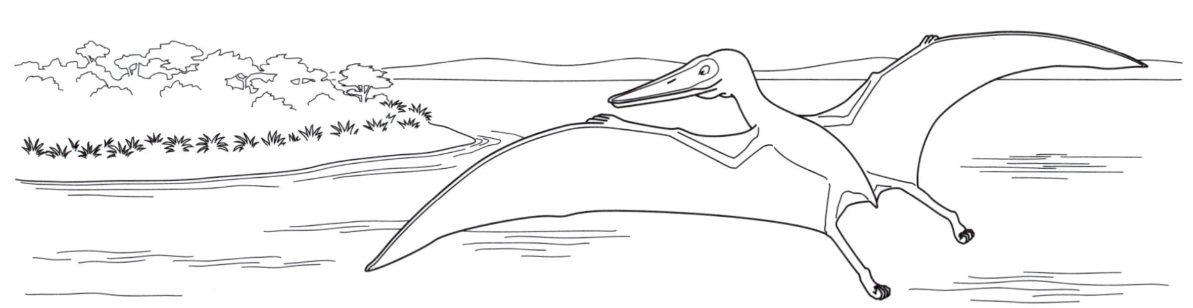

Trace.

ele ele ele ele ele

Trace and copy.

a a a a a a

a

A A A A A A

A

alone among afraid all

Find your best lower-case 'a' and place a tick neatly above it.
Do the same for your best capital 'A'.

Trace and copy.

Little Dinosaur was not

afraid. He knew he was

not alone. He was

among his friends.

Spelling tip

Do you want an easy way to remember how to spell the word 'friend'?

"I have a fri<u>end</u> until the <u>end</u>!"

Trace.

Trace and copy.

d d d d d d
d
D D D D D D
D

deep dinosaur disappear

Find your best lower-case 'd' and place a tick neatly above it.
Do the same for your best capital 'D'.

Trace and copy.

Small Duck-bill looked

for the other duck-bills.

Had they disappeared?

Punctuation practice

A question mark goes at the end of a question.

Find the question mark in the text above. Circle it neatly.

Trace some question marks of your own.

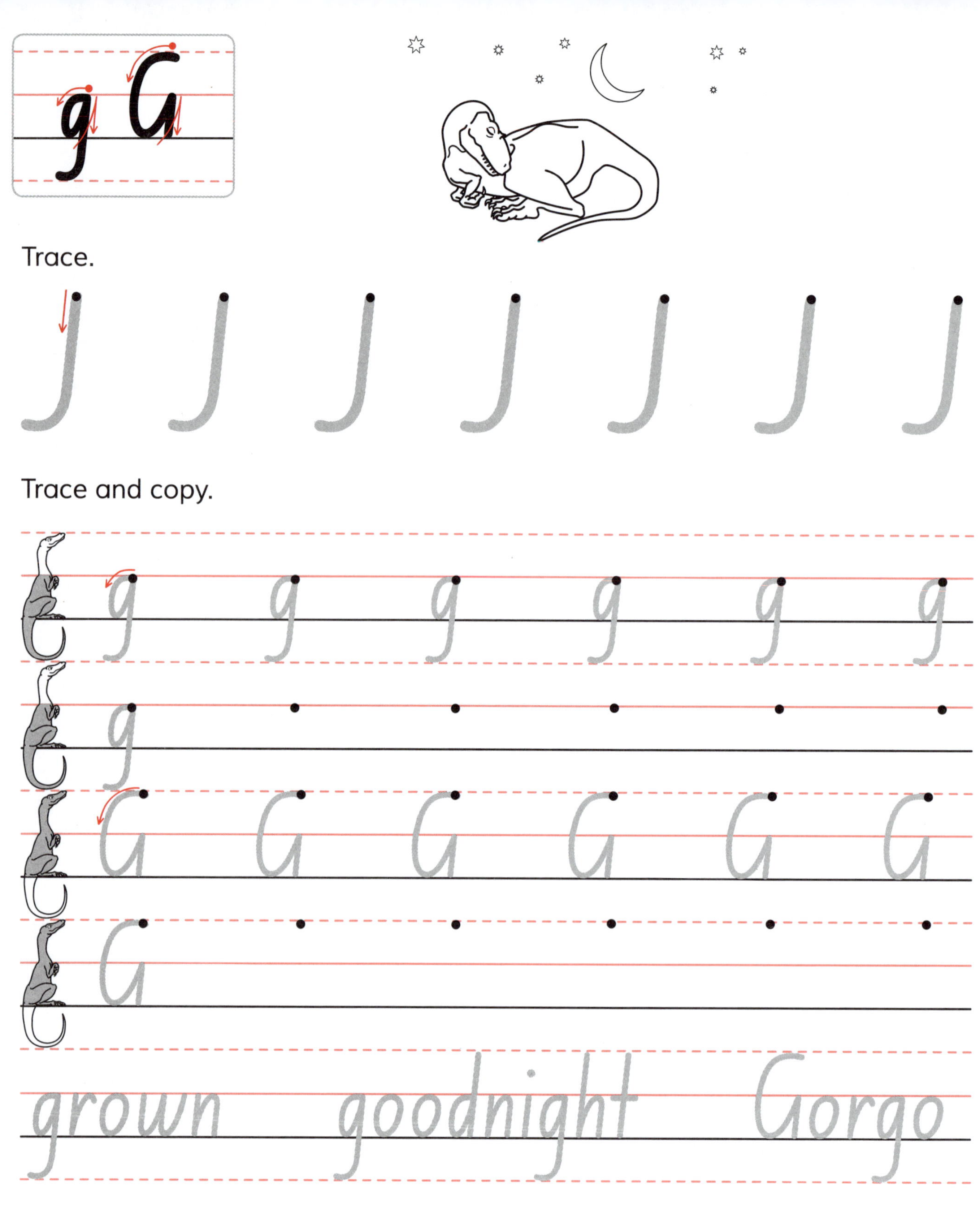

Find your best lower-case 'g' and place a tick neatly above it.
Do the same for your best capital 'G'.

Trace and copy.

Gorgo was big and strong.

Now she was fully grown,

she was nine metres long!

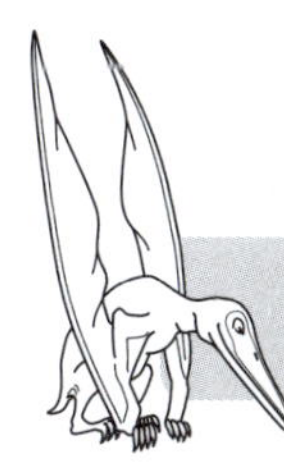

Punctuation practice

An exclamation mark goes at the end of a sentence to add emphasis or show strong feelings.

Find the exclamation mark in the text above. Circle it neatly.

Trace some exclamation marks of your own.

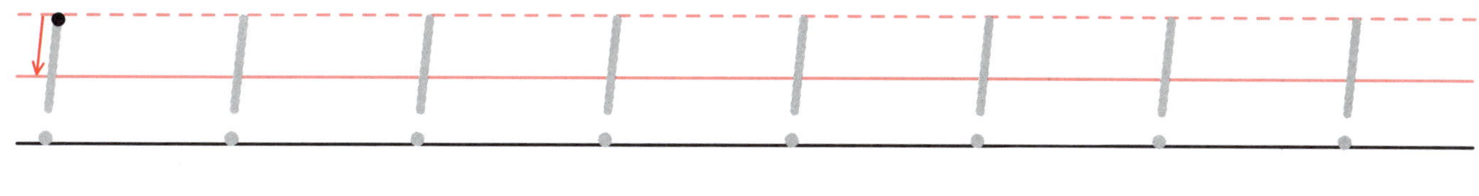

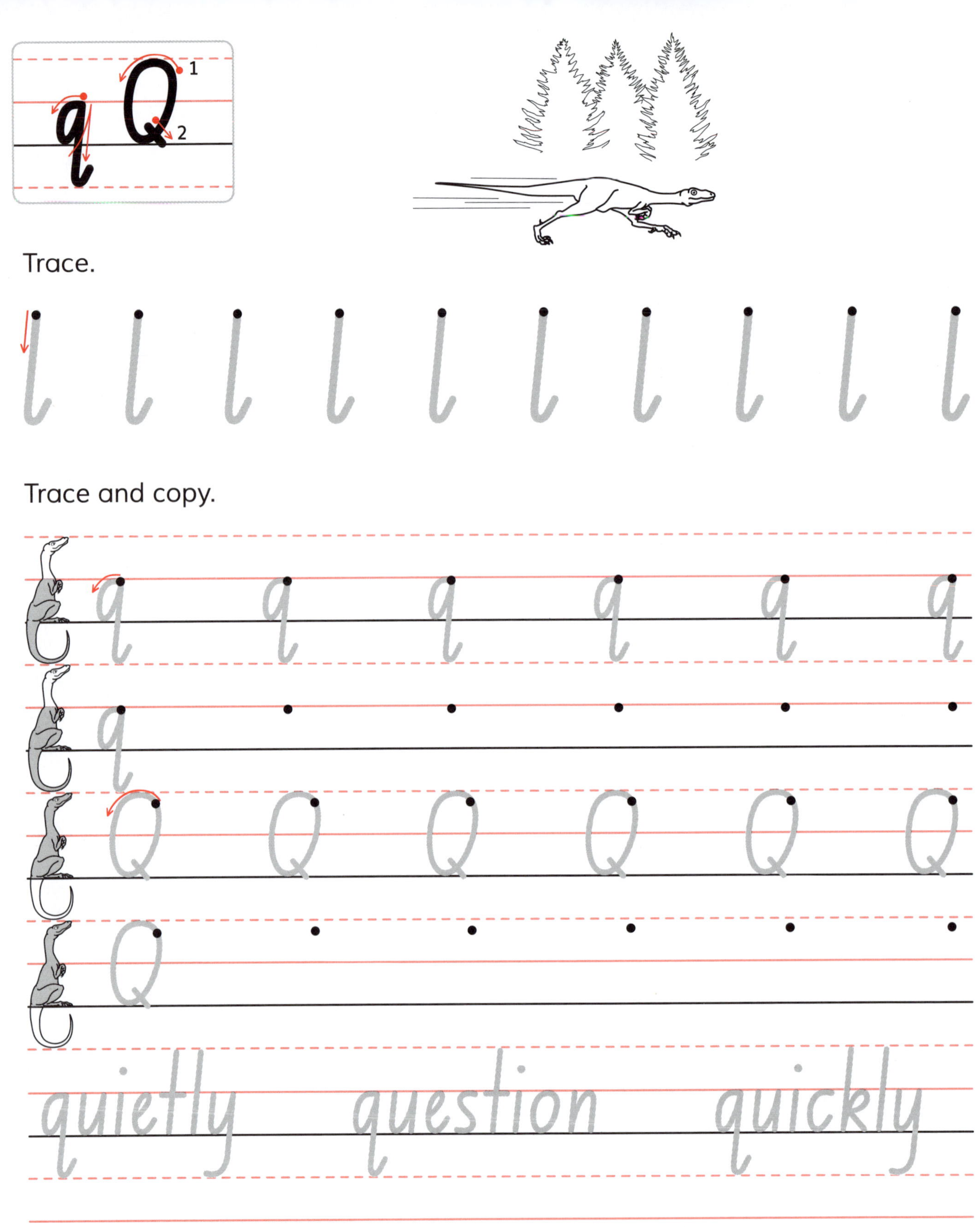

Find your best lower-case 'q' and place a tick neatly above it.
Do the same for your best capital 'Q'.

Trace and copy.

Q: Do you know which

Q:

animals are the closest

living relatives to dinosaurs?

A: b_r_s

A:

get.ga/PMWA71

Can you write a dinosaur question of your own?

Trace.

Trace and copy.

c c c c c c

c

C C C C C C

C

call carrots crocodile

Find your best lower-case 'c' and place a tick neatly above it.
Do the same for your best capital 'C'.

Trace and copy.

Q: What do you call a

Q:

stegosaurus with carrots

in its ears?

A: Anything you want.

A:

It can't hear you!

Trace.

ℓℓℓ ℓℓℓ ℓℓℓ ℓℓℓ ℓℓℓ

Trace and copy.

e e e e e e

e

E E E E E E

E

eggs empty eaten each

Find your best lower-case 'e' and place a tick neatly above it.
Do the same for your best capital 'E'.

Trace and copy.

Q: How many dinosaurs

Q:

can fit in an empty box?

A: One. After that, the

A:

box isn't empty any more!

Draw your favourite dinosaur inside the box.

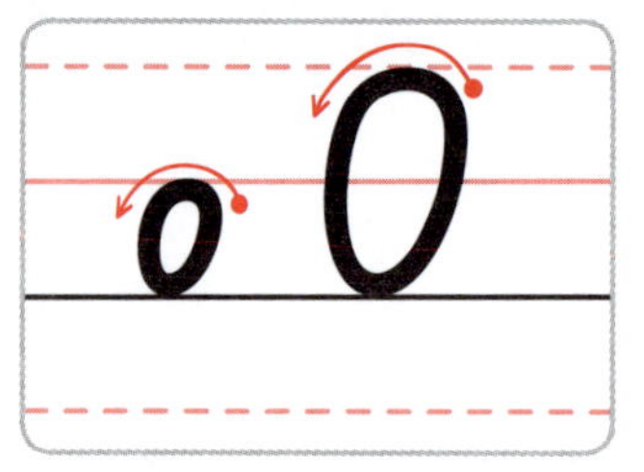

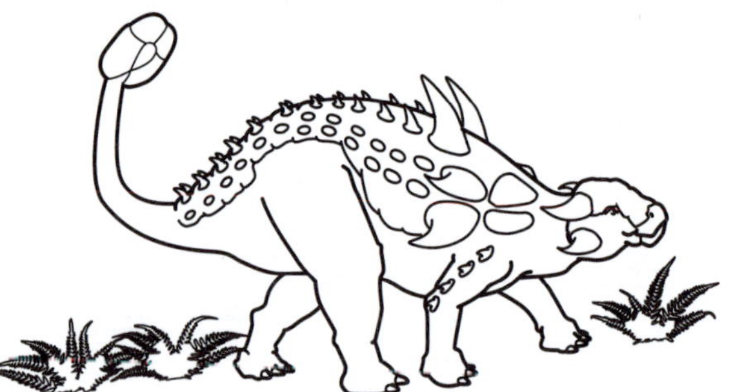

o O

Trace.

o o o o o o o o o

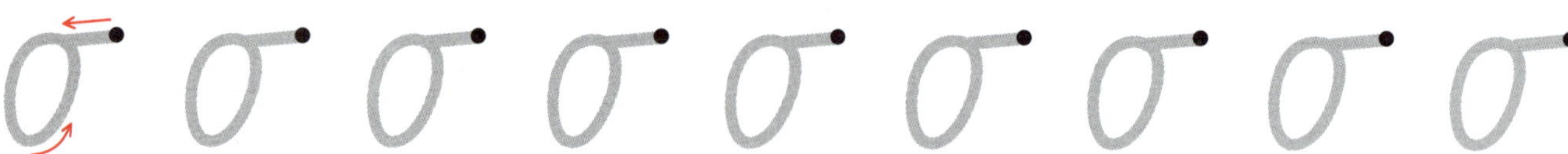

Trace and copy.

o o o o o o

o

O O O O O O

O

one outside often over

Find your best lower-case 'o' and place a tick neatly above it.
Do the same for your best capital 'O'.

Trace and copy the poem. Create your own ending on a new sheet of paper.

Dinosaur, dinosaur,

Turn around.

Dinosaur, dinosaur,

Stomp the ground!

Trace.

Trace and copy.

s s s s s s

s

S S S S S S

S

smell shake splashes she

Find your best lower-case 's' and place a tick neatly above it.
Do the same for your best capital 'S'.

Trace and copy.

get.ga/PMWA72

Q: What do you call a

Q:

fossil that doesn't ever

want to work?

A: Lazy bones!

A:

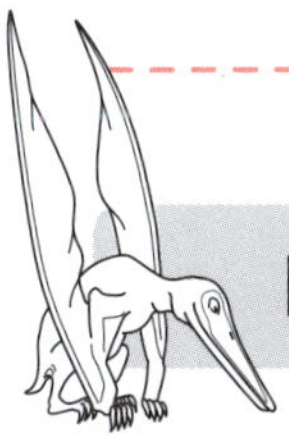

Punctuation practice

You can use an apostrophe to show where letters have been left out of a contraction.

Trace the following contractions. Draw neat circles around the apostrophes.

you're can't he's won't

Self-assessment: Anti-clockwise movement

Trace and copy.

u U y Y v V w W

a A d D g G q Q

c C e E o O s S

Circle the anti-clockwise letters in the word below. Colour all the wedges.

wingspan

Self-assessment

How neat are your anti-clockwise letters?

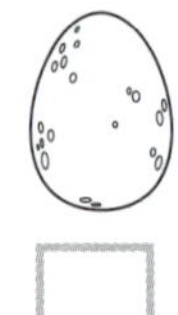
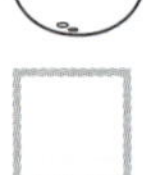

I need to work on these.

Good.

Great!

Clockwise movement

Try these clockwise patterns. Start at the dots. Follow the arrows.

Trace.

Trace and copy.

n n n n n n

n

N N N N N N

N

nest noise nearly night

Which letter have you traced or copied the most carefully?

Find your best lower-case 'n' and place a tick neatly above it.
Do the same for your best capital 'N'.

Trace and copy.

"Tyrannosaurus Rex is nearly here! Don't make a noise." The baby dinosaurs ran to hide in their nest.

Colour the wedges.

n n n n n n

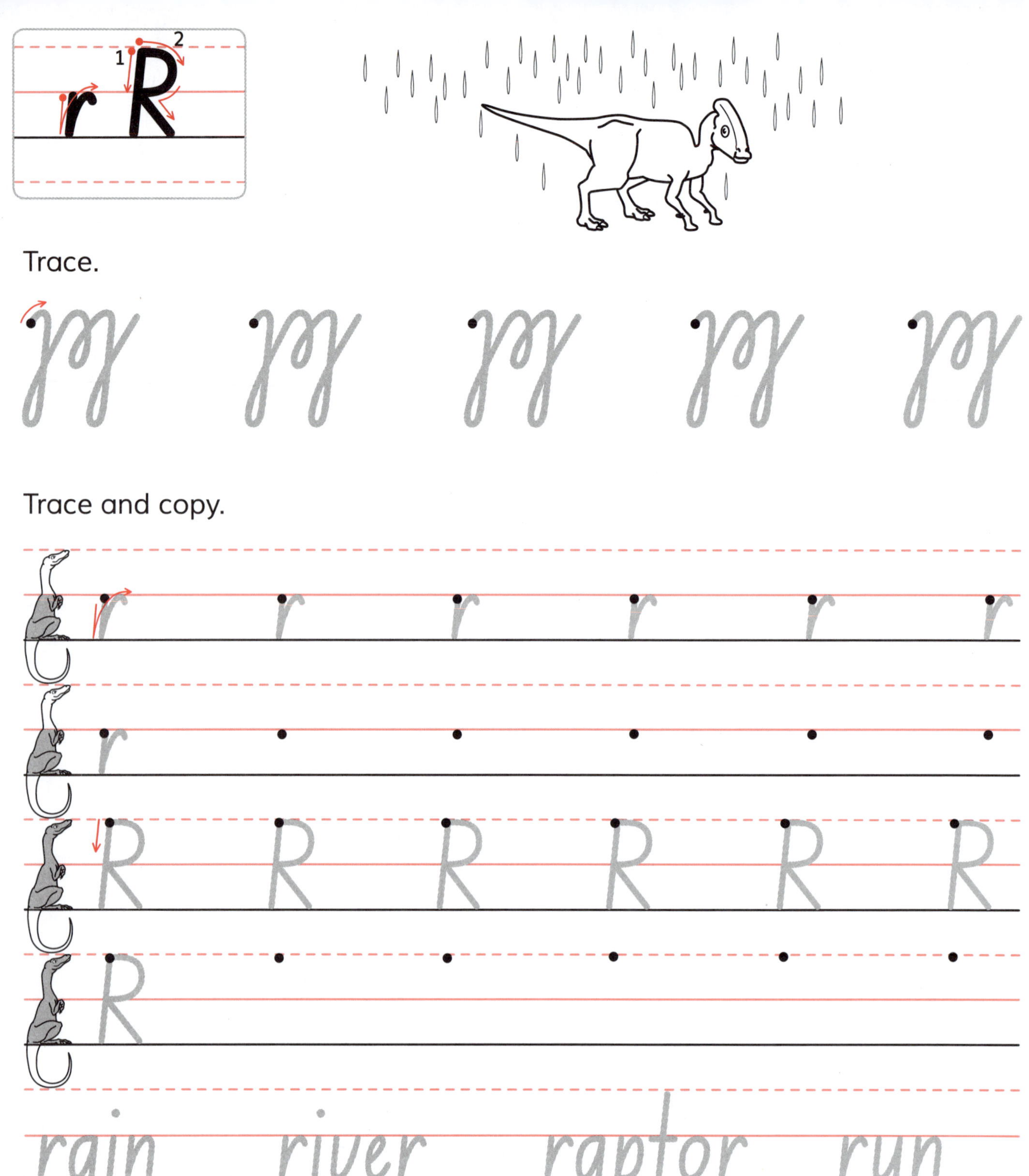

Trace.

Trace and copy.

r r r r r r

r

R R R R R R

R

rain river raptor run

Find your best lower-case 'r' and place a tick neatly above it.
Do the same for your best capital 'R'.

Trace and copy.

The raptor hurriedly tried

to cross the river before

the rain poured down.

Circle the letters with wedges in the sentence above. Colour the wedges.

Trace.

m m m m

Trace and copy.

m m m m m m

m

M M M M M M

M

mighty move meat-eater

Find your best lower-case 'm' and place a tick neatly above it.
Do the same for your best capital 'M'.

Trace and copy.

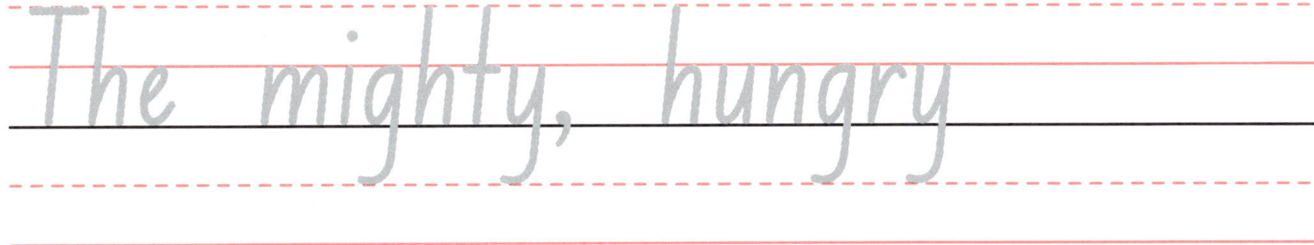

meat-eater was moving

through the trees.

Circle the letters with wedges in the sentence above. Colour the wedges.

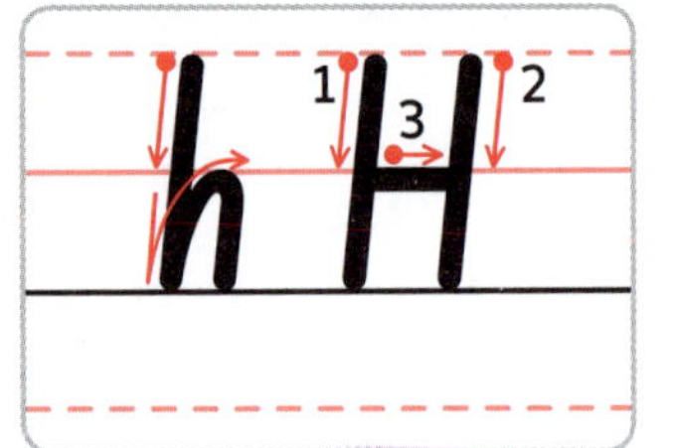

Trace.

h h h h h

Trace and copy.

h h h h h h

h

H H H H H H

H

huge happy herbivore hatch

Find your best lower-case 'h' and place a tick neatly above it.
Do the same for your best capital 'H'.

Trace and copy.

The baby herbivore

hatched from his egg.

His huge father was

happy to see him.

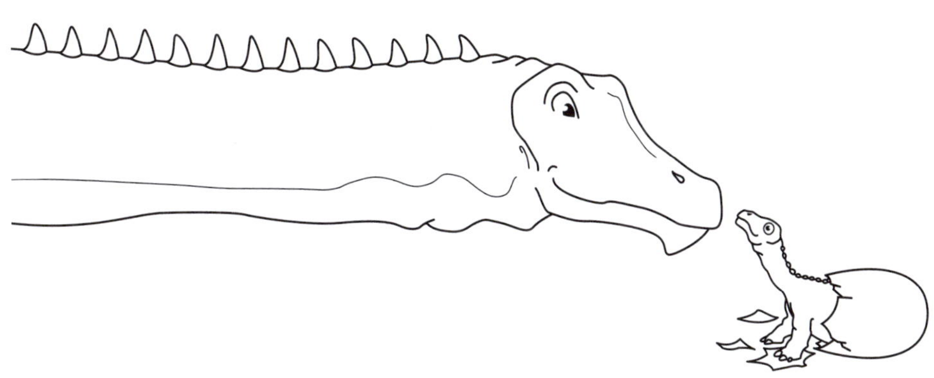

get.ga/PMWA73

Circle the letters with wedges in the sentence above. Colour the wedges.

Trace.

Trace and copy.

k k k k k k

k

K K K K K K

K

kick knocked knee kind

Find your best lower-case 'k' and place a tick neatly above it.
Do the same for your best capital 'K'.

Trace and copy.

The apatosauruses kicked

their legs until they knew

they were safely across

the lake.

Spelling tip

The letter 'k' is sometimes silent.

Draw a circle around the silent 'k' in the sentence above.

Some other words with silent 'k': knee, knock, knit, knot.

Trace.

Trace and copy.

b b b b b b

b

B B B B B B

B

baby broke born be

Find your best lower-case 'b' and place a tick neatly above it.
Do the same for your best capital 'B'.

Trace and copy.

Baby dinosaur broke

through the eggshell on

the day she was born.

Colour the wedges.

b d h k n g y

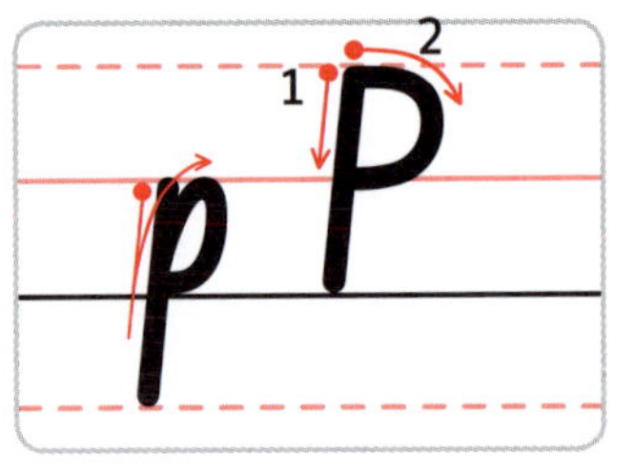

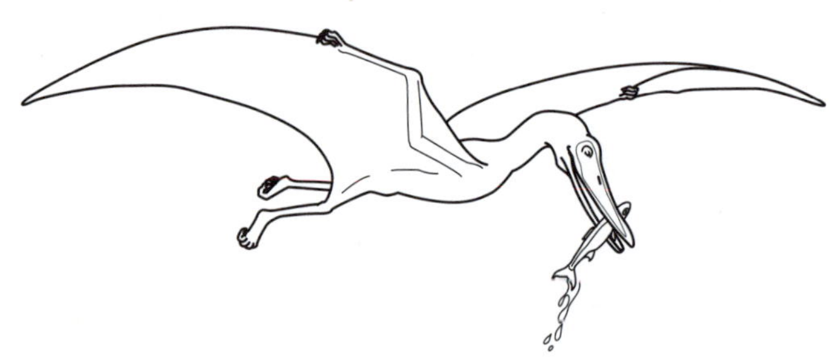

Trace.

r r r r r r r

Trace and copy.

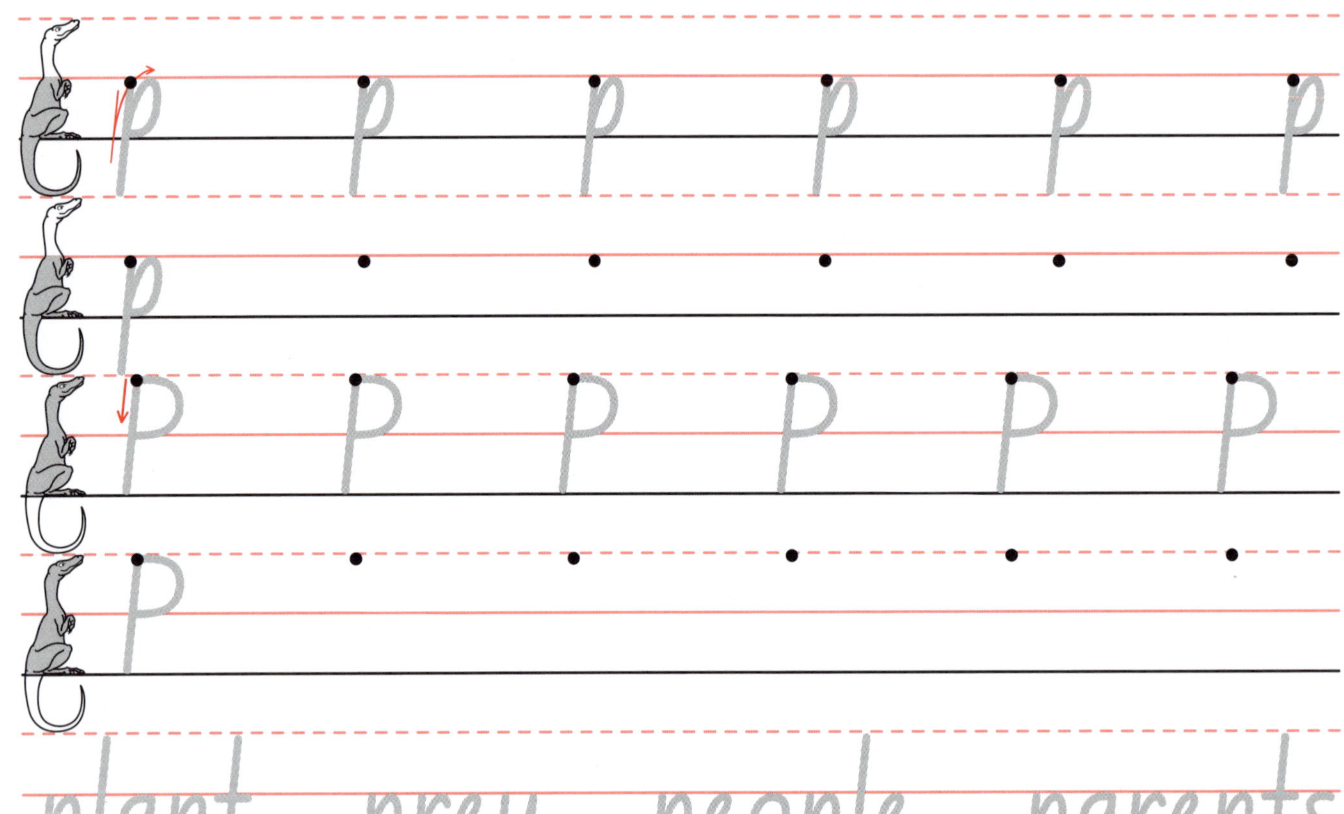

plant prey people parents

Find your best lower-case 'p' and place a tick neatly above it.
Do the same for your best capital 'P'.

Trace and copy.

Before there were any

people, there were

dinosaurs. Some chased

their prey and others

were plant-eaters.

Circle the letters with wedges in the text above.
Colour the wedges.

Self-assessment: Clockwise movement

Trace and copy.

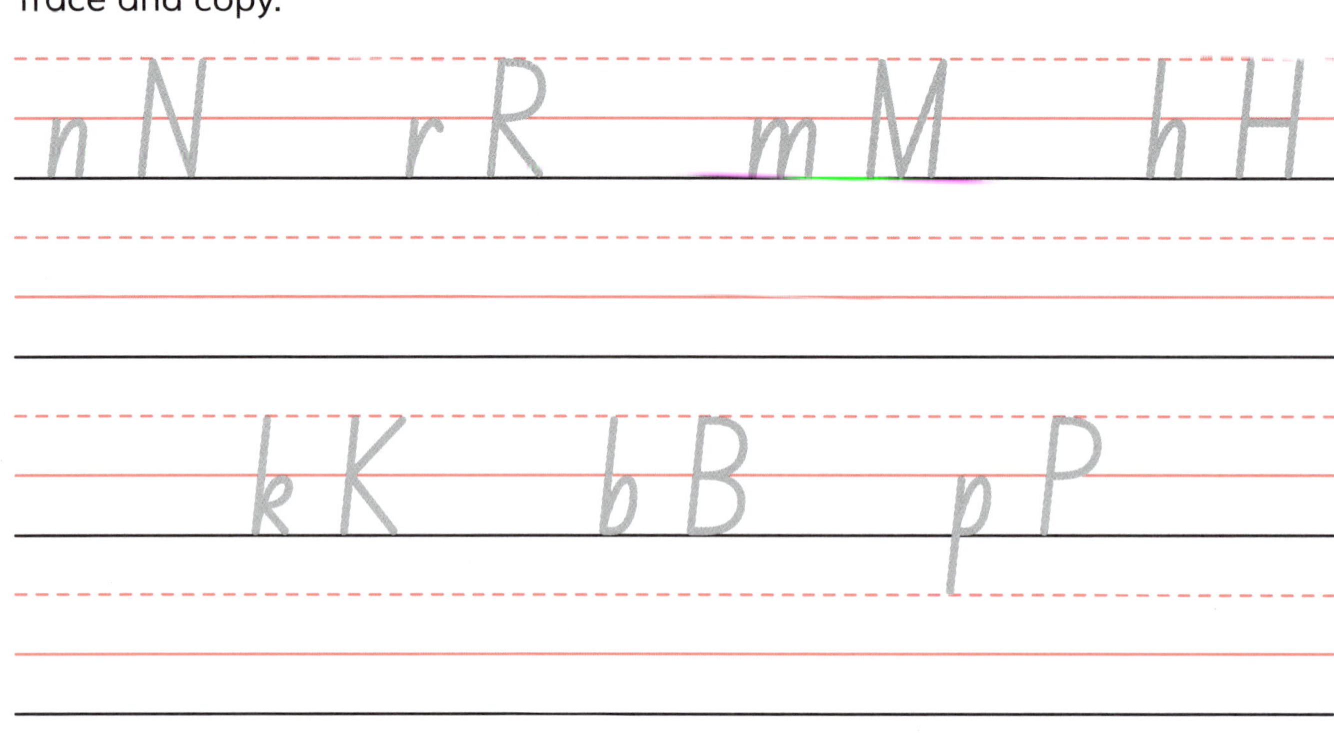

Circle the 4 clockwise letters in the word below, then colour the wedges.

Tyrannosaurus

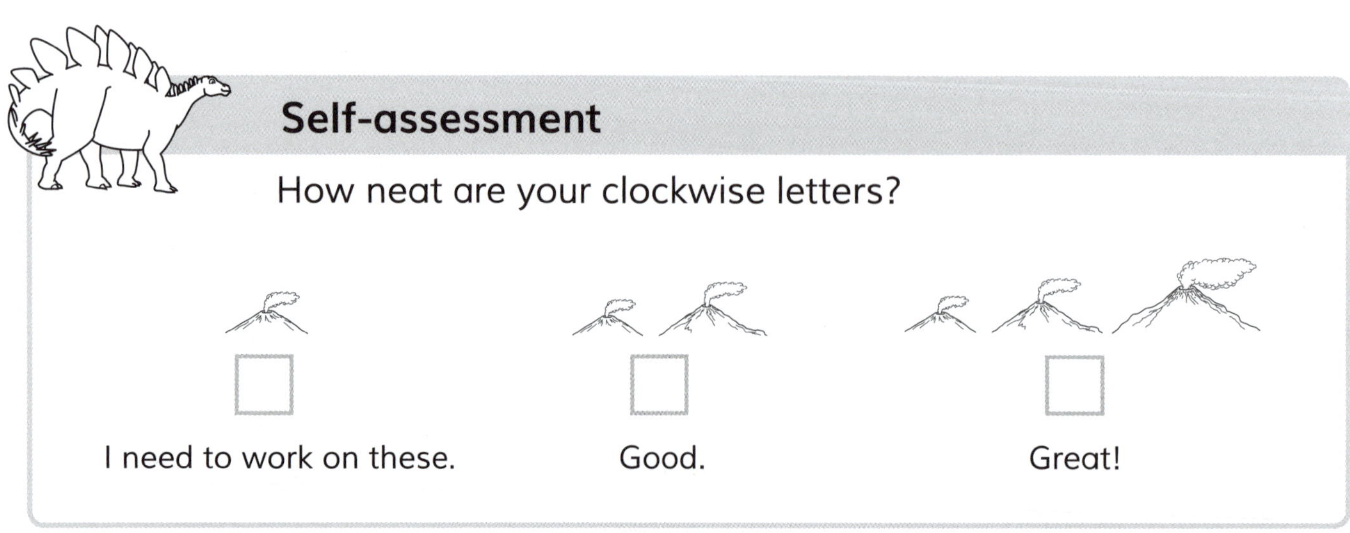

Downstroke movement

Try these downstroke patterns. Start at the dots. Follow the arrows.

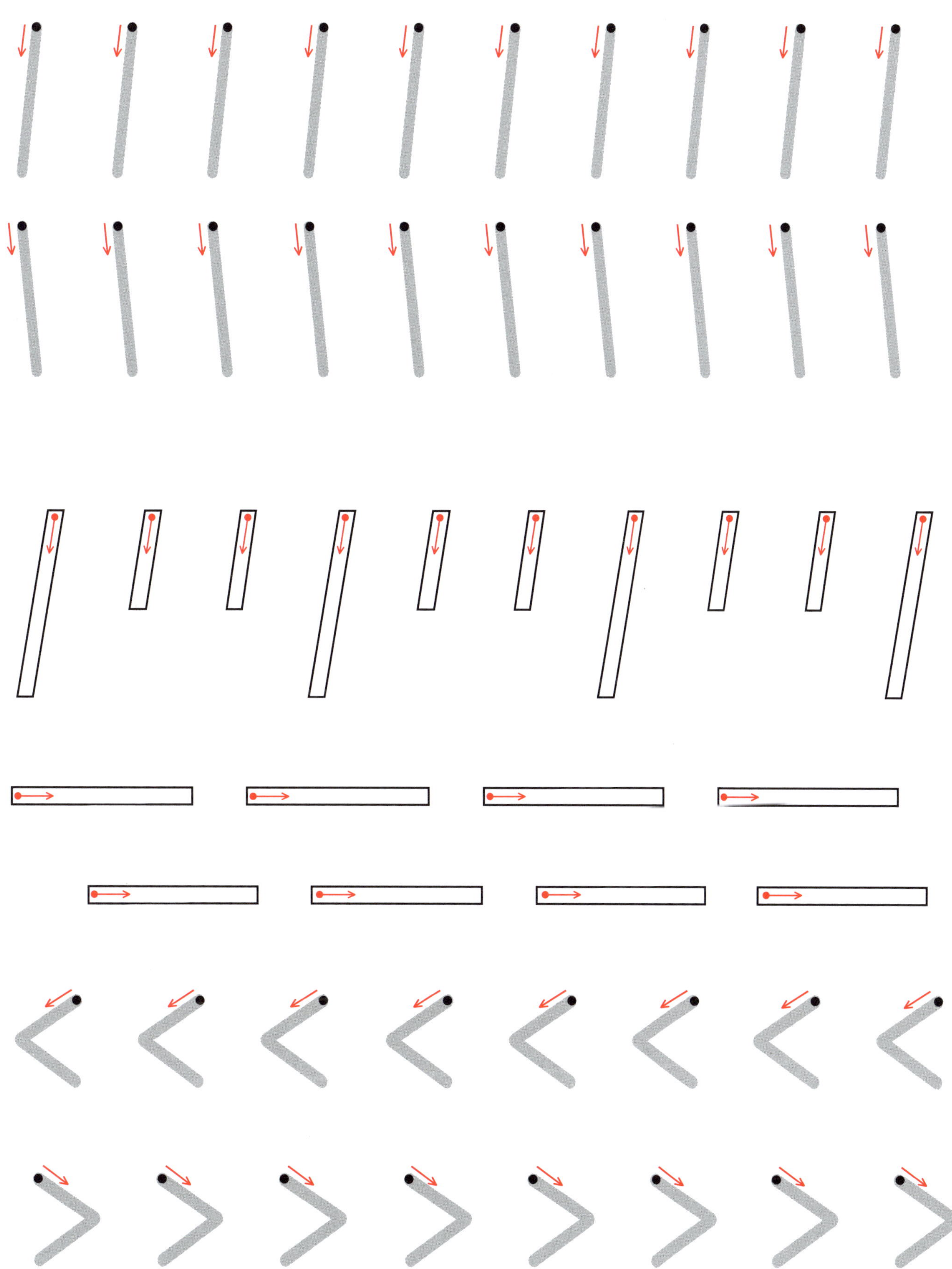

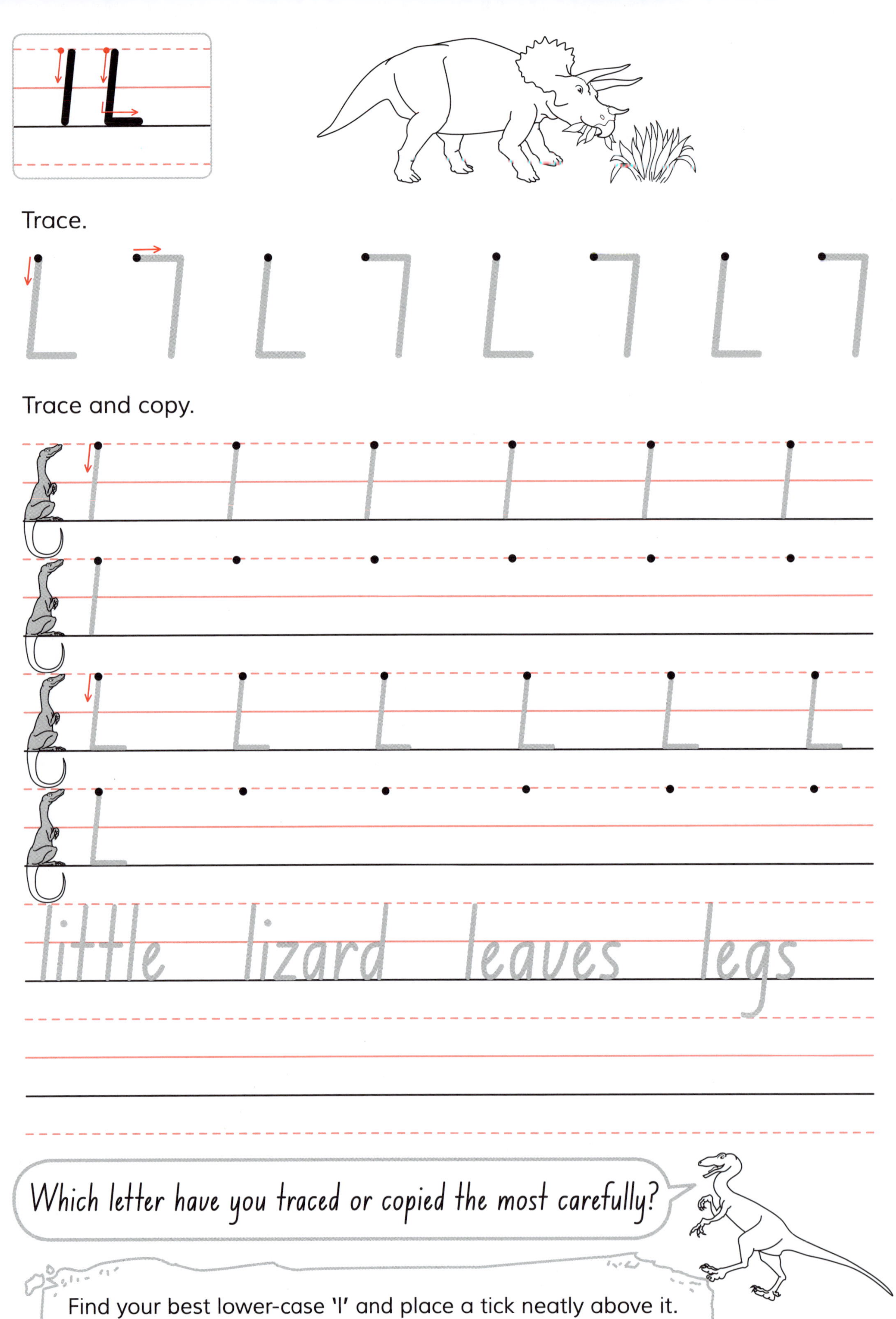

Find your best lower-case 'l' and place a tick neatly above it.
Do the same for your best capital 'L'.

Trace and copy.

Trace the leaf shapes.

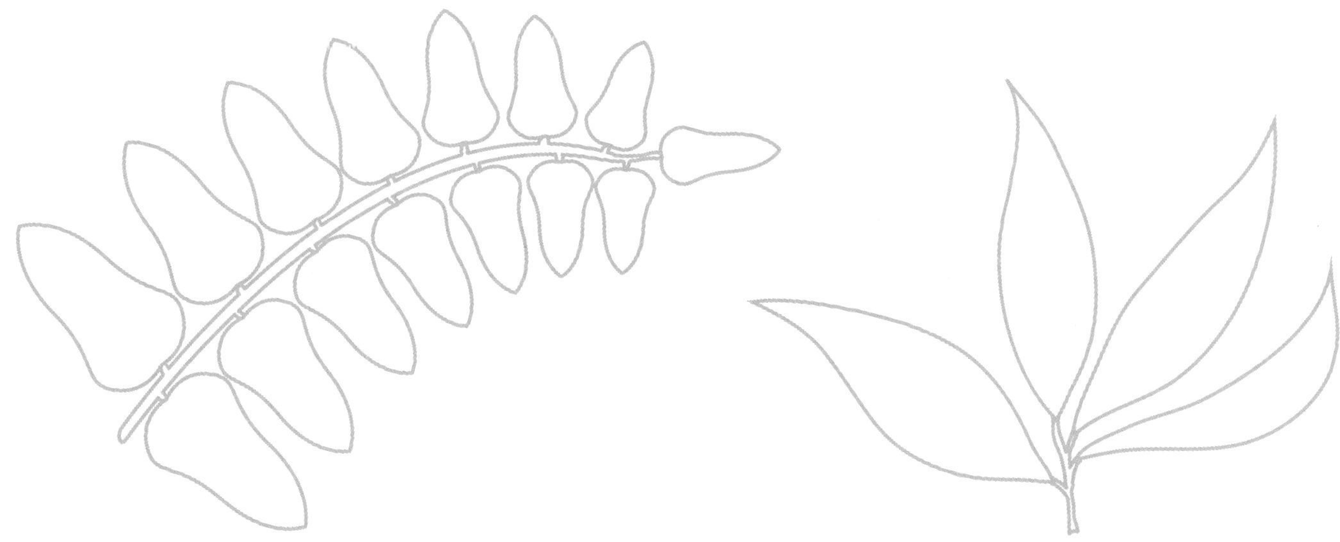

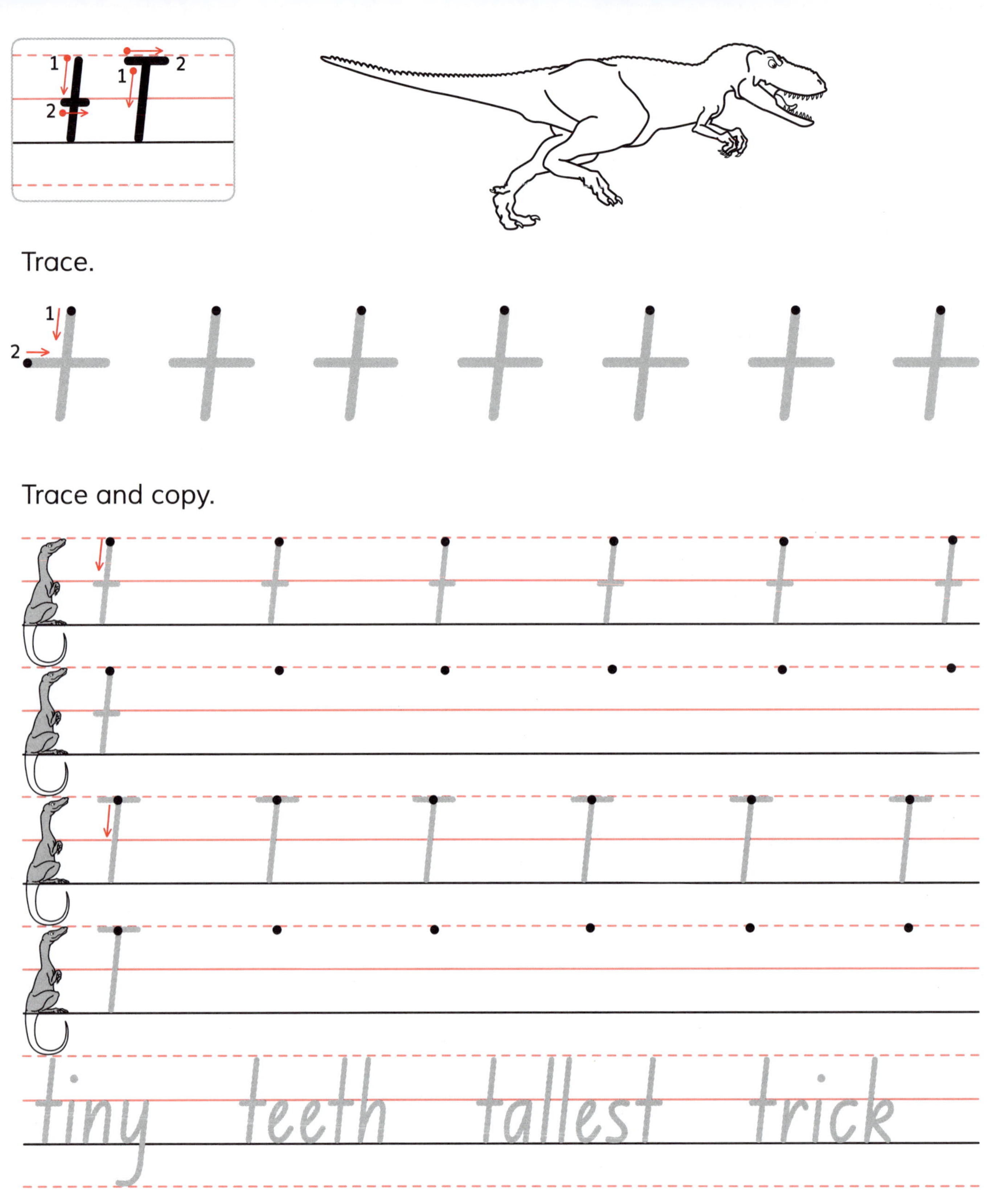

Trace.

Trace and copy.

Find your best lower-case 't' and place a tick neatly above it.
Do the same for your best capital 'T'.

Trace and copy.

Tyrannosaurus Rex had

big teeth, but brave

Triceratops did not tremble.

There are 16 letters in the words 'Tyrannosaurus Rex'. How many letters are in the word 'Triceratops'? Complete the sum to find out, then check by counting.

3 + 3 + 4 + 1 = ______

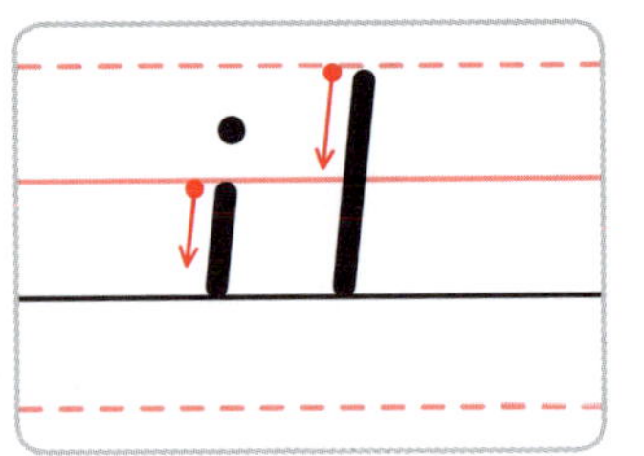

Trace.

Trace and copy.

in important inside its

Find your best lower-case 'i' and place a tick neatly above it.
Do the same for your best capital 'I'.

Trace and copy.

Little Dinosaur raced into

the cave, just in time.

The letter 'i' is a vowel. There are five vowels: a, e, i, o and u. Draw neat circles around each vowel in the sentence above.

Trace.

Trace and copy.

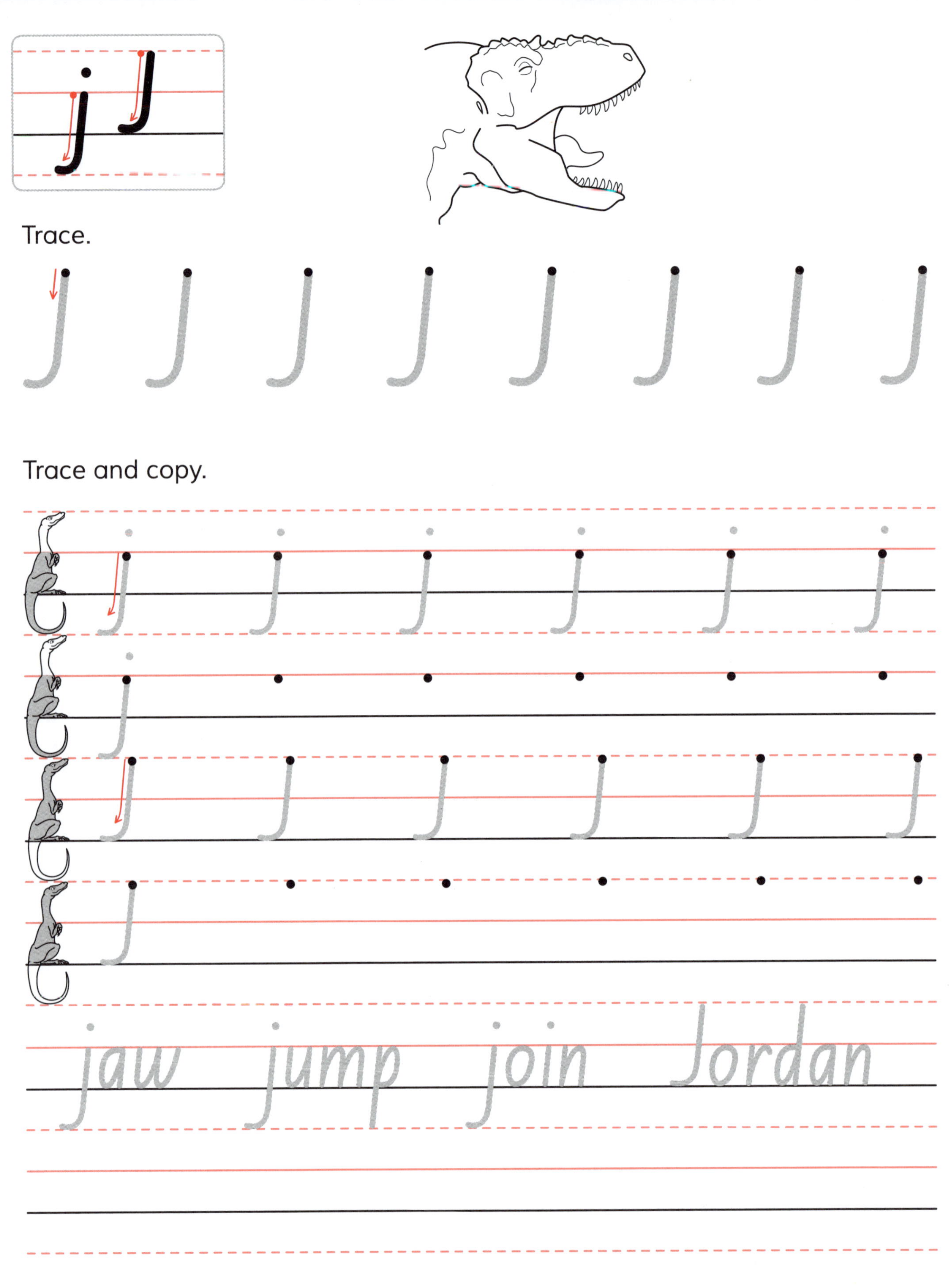

Find your best lower-case 'j' and place a tick neatly above it.
Do the same for your best capital 'J'.

Trace and copy.

enjoy jaw jelly

banjo jump join

Can you neatly rewrite the words above in alphabetical order?

Clue: When the first letter is the same, use the next letter to decide alphabetical order.

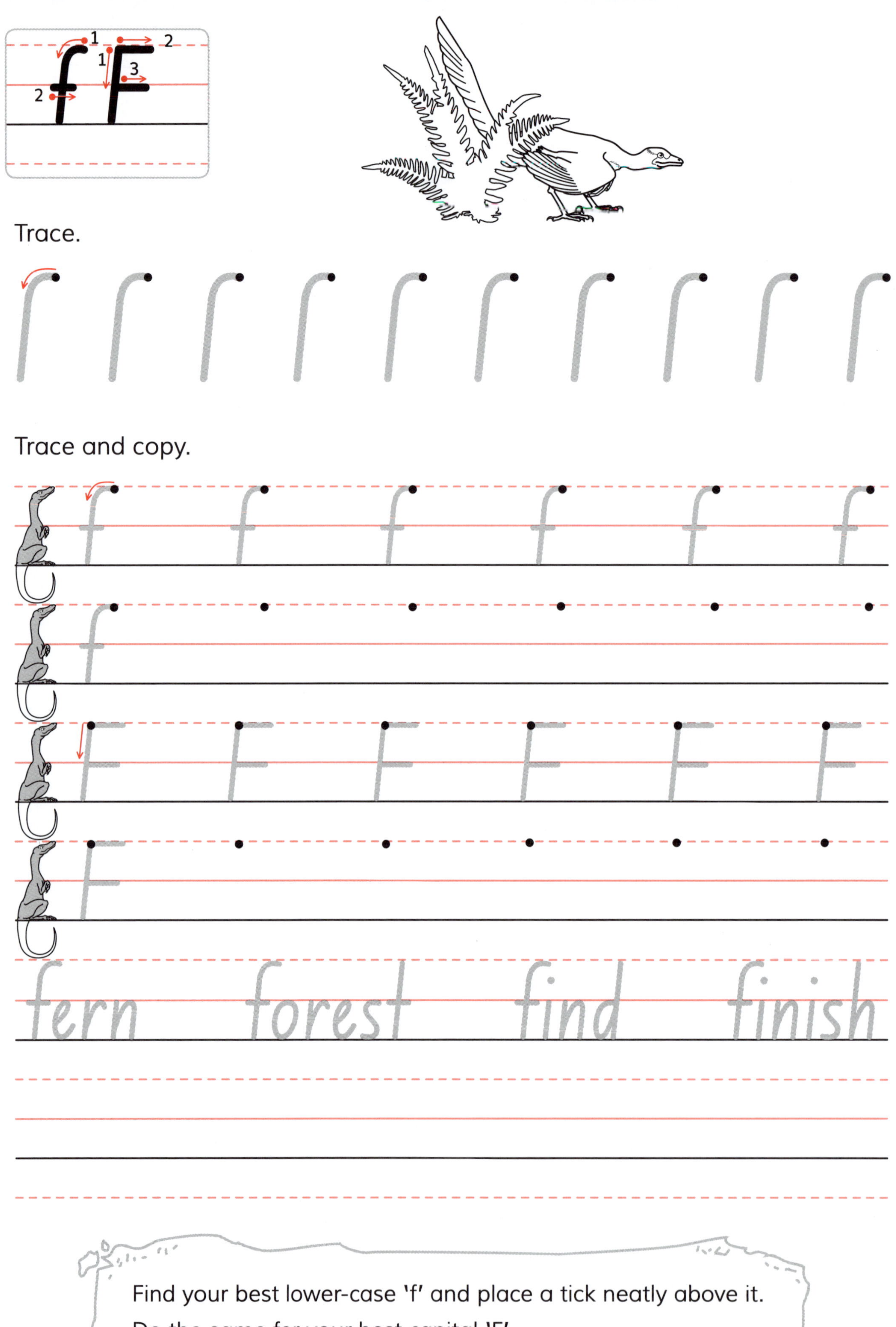

Find your best lower-case 'f' and place a tick neatly above it.
Do the same for your best capital 'F'.

Trace and copy.

The triceratops had to go

far away from the forest

to forage for food.

Draw a neat circle around every letter 'f' in the sentence above.

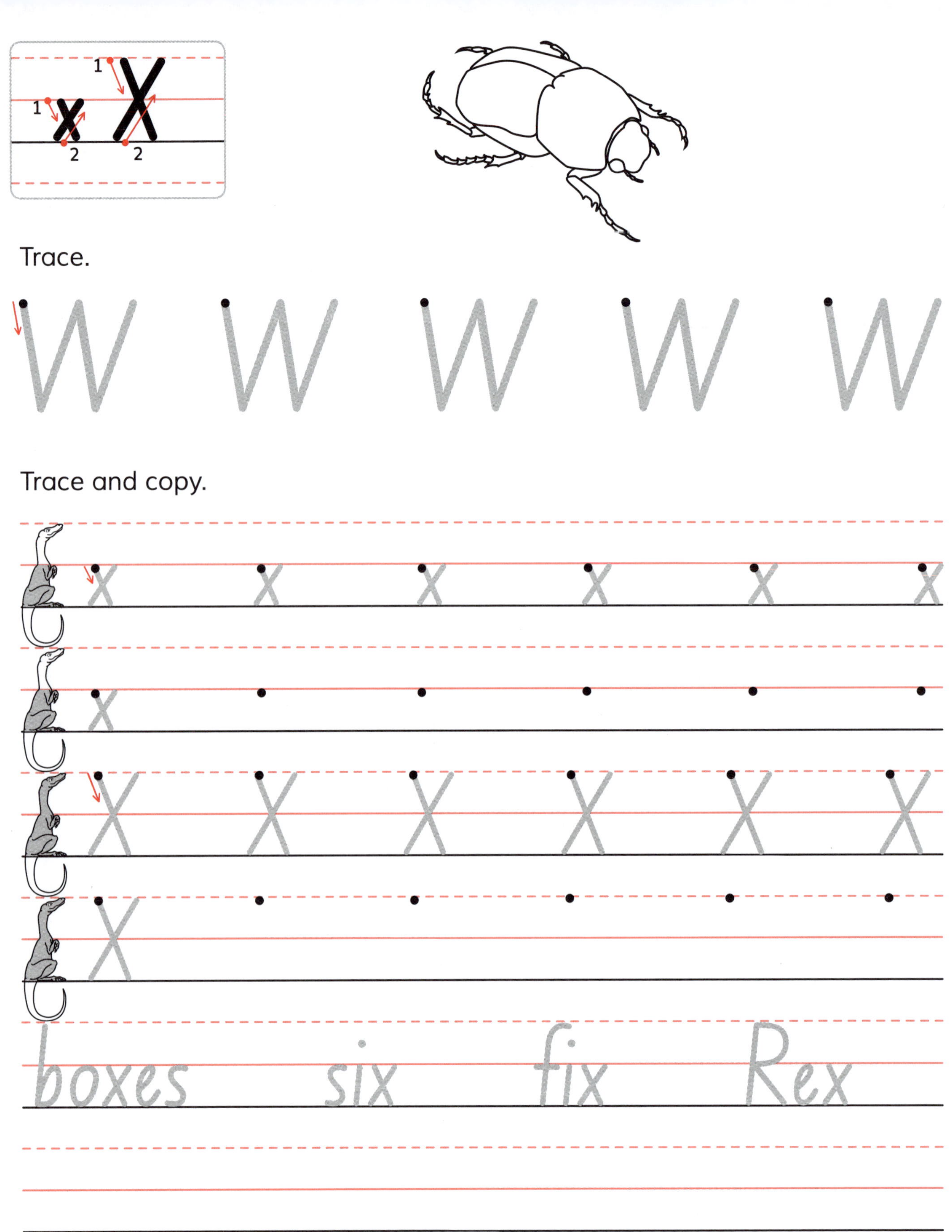

Find your best lower-case 'x' and place a tick neatly above it.
Do the same for your best capital 'X'.

Trace and copy.

"Go away, Tyrannosaurus Rex,

so we can fix our nest!" said

the six baby dinosaurs.

Punctuation practice

Speech marks, or quotation marks, are used to show when someone is speaking. They always come in pairs.

Draw neat circles around the speech marks on this page.

Trace.

Trace and copy.

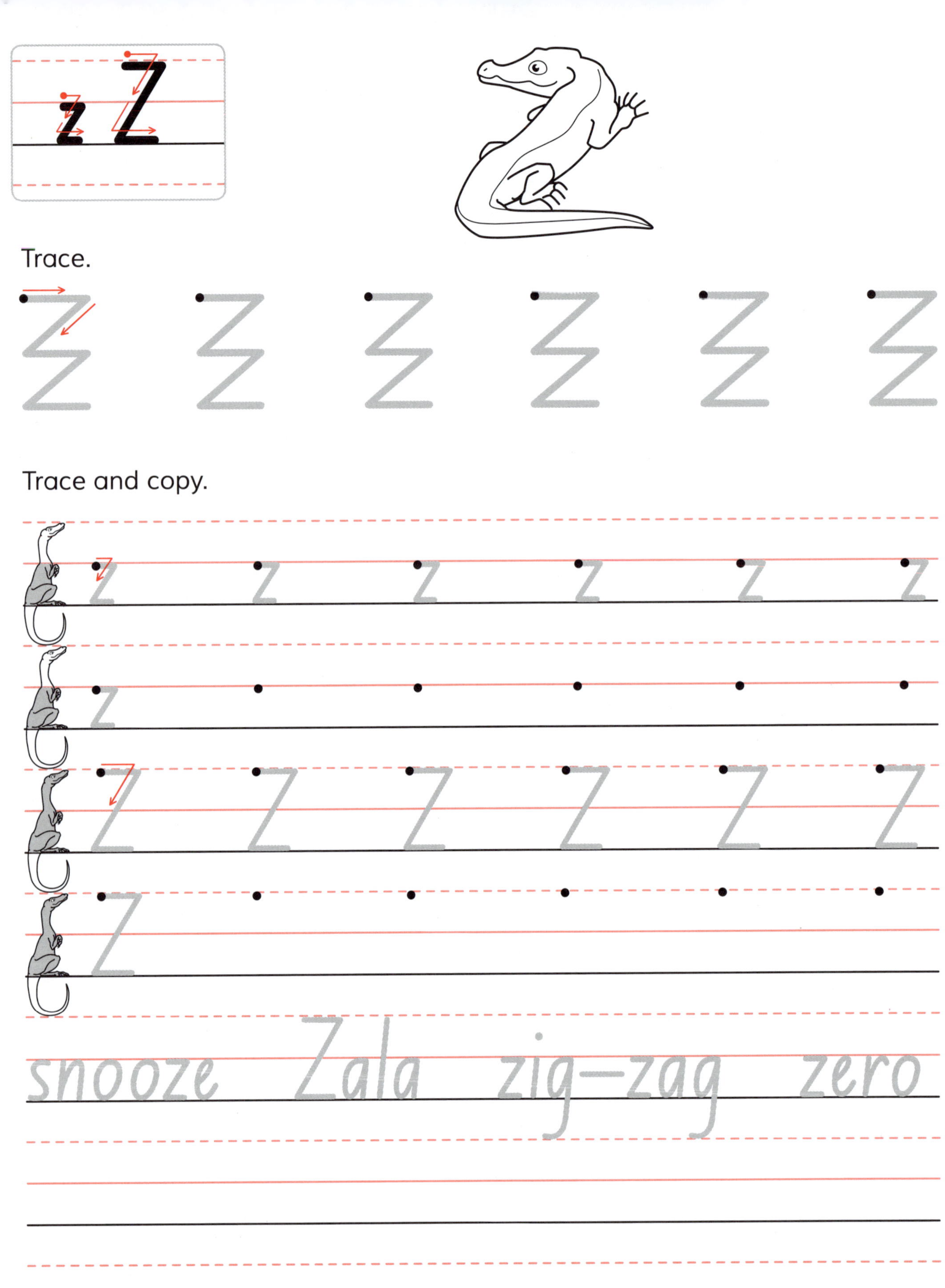

Find your best lower-case 'z' and place a tick neatly above it.
Do the same for your best capital 'Z'.

Trace and copy.

"I think you are amazing,"

Zala whispered to her six

snoozing babies.

get.ga/PMWA76

Trace the following sums and fill in the missing numbers.

Ten minus ____ equals zero.

Eight minus ____

equals four.

Self-assessment: Downstroke movement

Trace and copy.

lL tT iI jJ

fF xX zZ

Write the lower-case downstroke letters in the order they appear in the alphabet. The starting dots will give you clues.

f

Self-assessment

How neat are your downstroke letters?

☐ I need to work on these.

☐ Good.

☐ Great!

Numerals

Trace and copy.

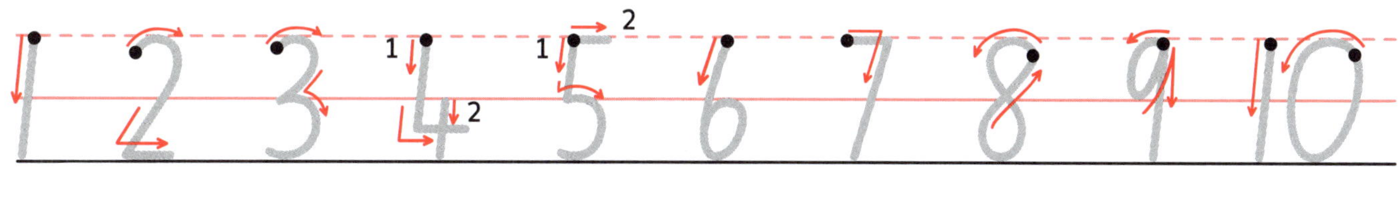

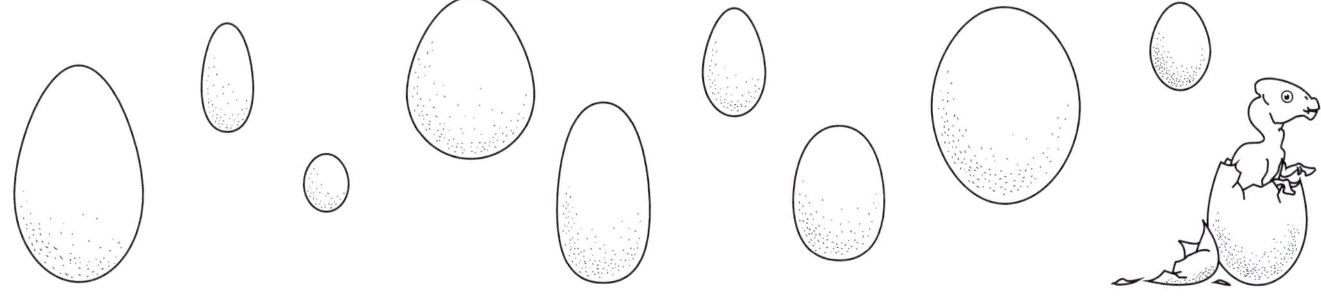

Trace the numbers.

10 ten 20 twenty

30 thirty 40 forty

50 fifty 60 sixty

70 seventy 80 eighty

90 ninety

100 one hundred

Alphabet review

Trace and copy the lower-case and capital letters in alphabetical order.

aA bB cC dD

eE fF gG hH

iI jJ kK lL

mM nN oO pP

qQ rR sS tT

uU vV wW xX

yY zZ

get.ga/PMWA77

Teacher observation guide

Student is: left handed ☐ right handed ☐

Student demonstrates correct posture, paper position and pencil grip. ☐

Student is stroking from top to bottom. ☐

Student is stroking from left to right. ☐

Student is tracking and tracing patterns correctly using starting dots and arrows. ☐

Student is tracing letters correctly using starting dots and arrows. ☐

Student forms lower-case letters of a consistent size with accuracy:

a	b	c	d	e	f	g	h	i	j	k	l	m	n	o	p	q	r	s	t	u	v	w	x	y	z

Student forms capital letters of a consistent size with accuracy:

A	B	C	D	E	F	G	H	I	J	K	L	M	N	O	P	Q	R	S	T	U	V	W	X	Y	Z

Student uses head, body and tail character to describe the spatial properties of letters. ☐

Student can copy a word with accuracy. ☐

Student can copy a complete sentence with accuracy. ☐

Student is placing letters correctly within lines. ☐

Student can identify which movement group letters belong to (anti-clockwise, clockwise, downstroke). ☐

Student can identify and colour wedges ☐

Student can write numerals 1–100. ☐

Student can self-assess with accuracy. ☐

Notes:

....

....

Date: ....

CERTIFICATE

get.ga/PMWC70